P9-CRA-695

A is for...?

A

is for...?

A PHOTOGRAPHER'S ALPHABET OF ANIMALS

Henry Horenstein

Gulliver Books
Harcourt Brace & Company
SAN DIEGO   NEW YORK   LONDON

Requests for permission to make copies of any part of the work should be mailed to: Permissions Department, Harcourt Brace & Company, 6277 Sea Harbor Drive, Orlando, Florida 32887-6777.

Gulliver Books is a registered trademark of Harcourt Brace & Company.

Library of Congress Cataloging-in-Publication Data
Horenstein, Henry.
A is for . . . ?: a photographer's alphabet of animals/by Henry Horenstein.
p. cm.
"Gulliver Books."
Summary: With the letters of the alphabet as clues, readers are challenged to guess the identity of the animals pictured in the photographs.
ISBN 0-15-201582-5
1. Animals—Pictorial works—Juvenile literature.   2. Alphabet—Juvenile literature.
3. Picture puzzles—Juvenile literature.   [1. Animals.   2. Alphabet.   3. Picture puzzles.]
I. Title.
TR727.H65   1999
590—dc21   98-31424

F E D C B

PRINTED IN HONG KONG

The photographs in this book were taken with Canon EOS camera bodies and lenses ranging from 14 mm to 1000 mm. Agfa Scala transparency film was used, and the photographs were printed on Ilfochrome and platinum paper.
The type was set in Caslon 3.
Color separations by Bright Arts Ltd., Hong Kong
Printed by South China Printing Company, Ltd., Hong Kong
This book was printed on totally chlorine-free Nymolla Matte Art paper.
Production supervision by Stanley Redfern
Designed by Kaelin Chappell

The author gratefully acknowledges the contributions of Frank Blasdell; David Caron; Kaelin Chappell; Anne Davies; Noe DeWitt; Megan Doyle; Kathleen Ewing Gallery, New York; Ann Fleisher; Pablo Garcia; Tom Gearty; Ginsburg/Hallowell Fine Art, Boston; Ann Grillo; Nina Hess; Robert Klein Gallery, Boston; Jessica Krumpen; Andy Morrison; Sarah Morthland Gallery, New York; Maggie North; Photonica, New York/Tokyo; The Platinum Gallery, New York; Andrea Raynor; Dawn Richfield; Linda Rohr; Susan Titus; Amy Townsend-Small; Dot Wensink; and ZONA, Cambridge.

Cover and title page answers: alligator

For Lisa De Francis

A

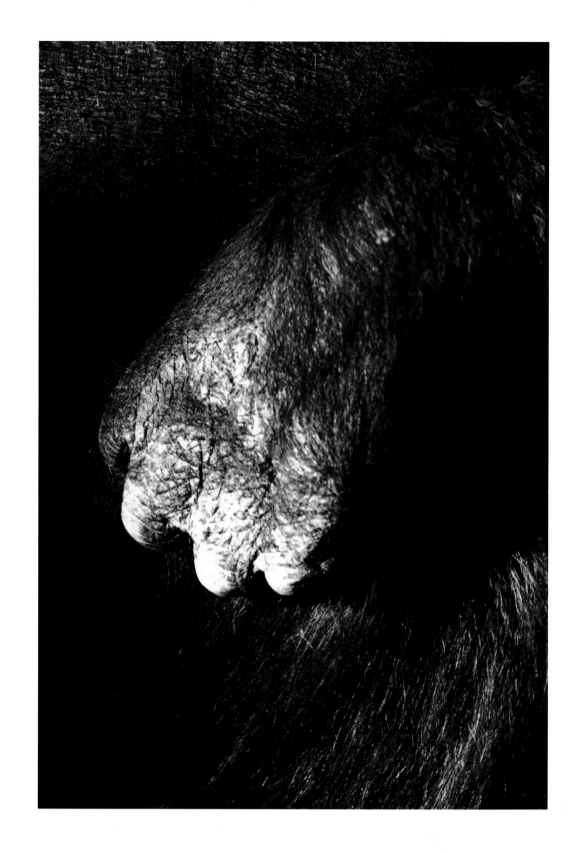

B

D

E

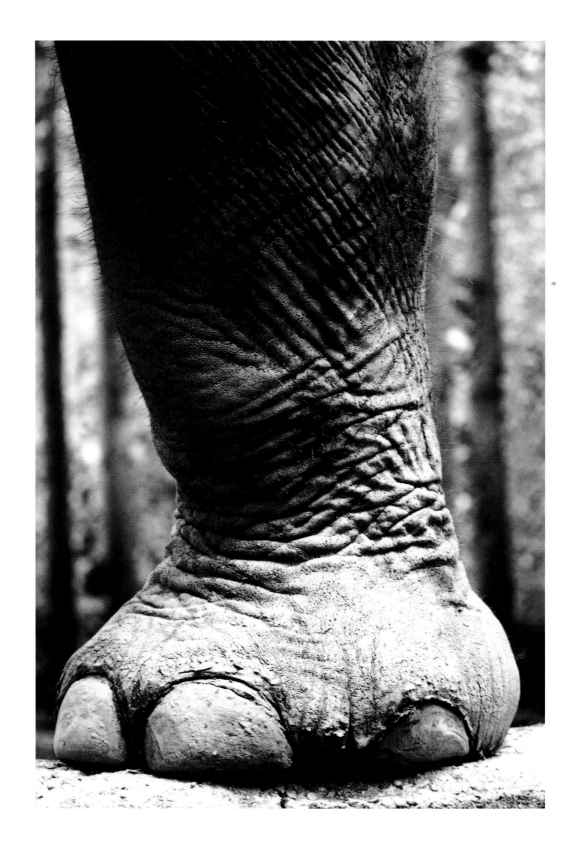

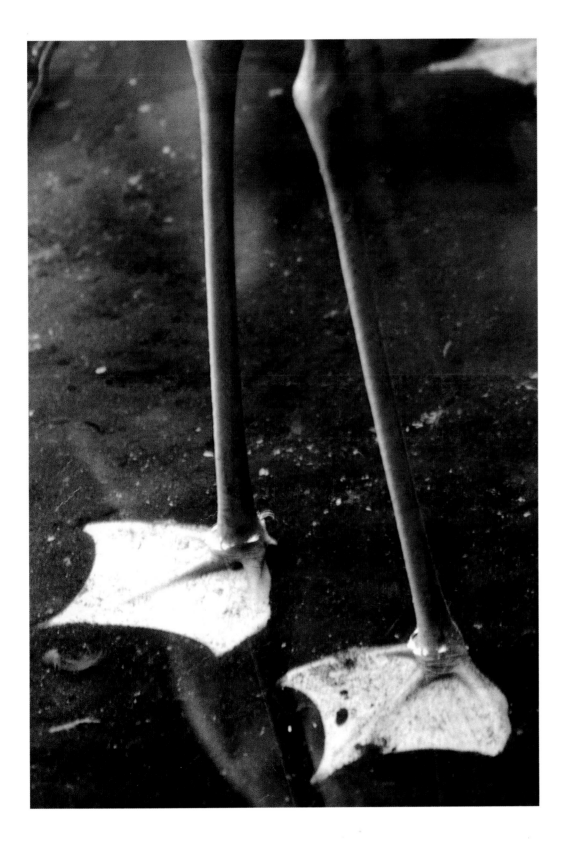

F

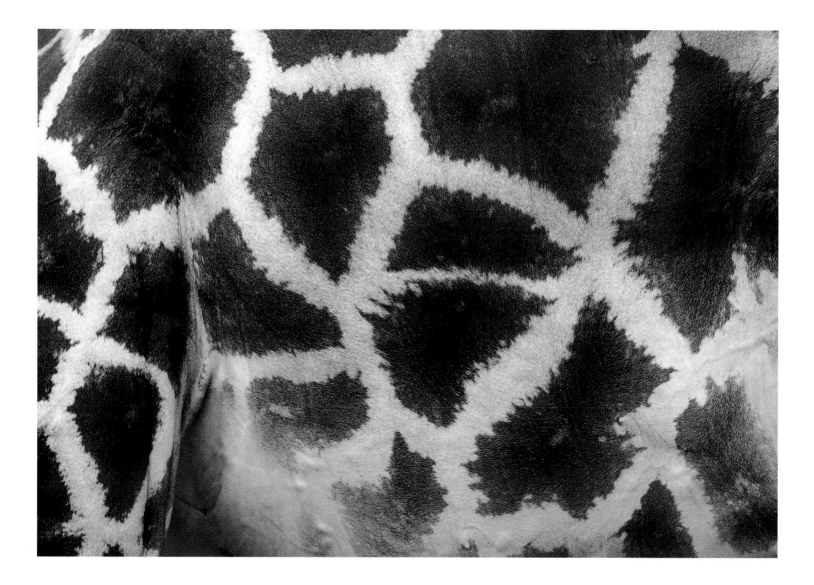

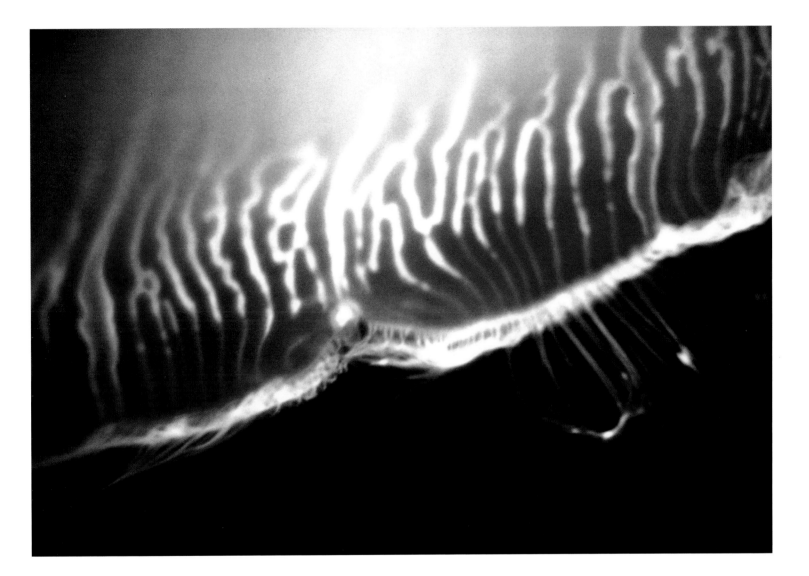

J

M

N

O

P

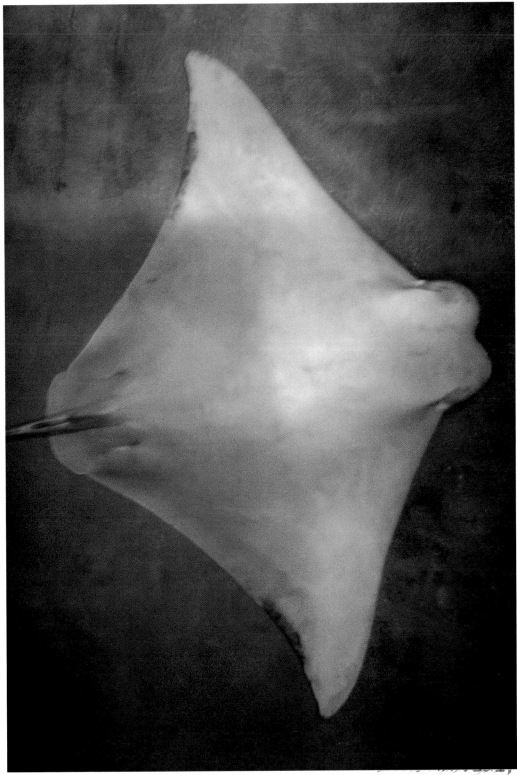

R

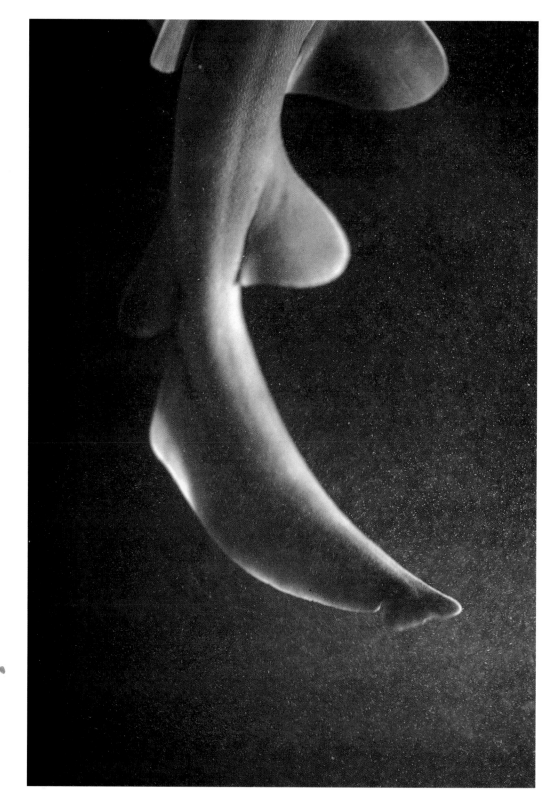

S

U

A is for… Answers

Ape

Bat

Cheetah

Duck

Elephant

Flamingo

Giraffe

Horse

Iguana

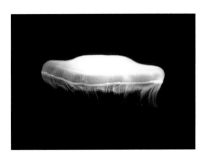

Jellyfish

Kudu

Lion

Monkey

Newt

Ostrich

Parrot

Quail

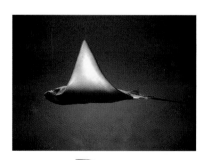

Ray

Shark

Tortoise

Urchin

Vulture

Whale

oX

Yellow Jacket

Zebra

Photographer's Note

Photographing wild animals is very different from photographing people. You can't tell a gorilla where to stand, and you can't ask an alligator to smile or a cheetah to say "cheese." Instead, you must be very patient and wait, hoping the animal will do what you want it to do—or something else unexpected that might make a good picture. When animals do cooperate, you have to be ready, because most won't stay in any one position long. You may have only a few seconds or less to get your shot.

It's sometimes hard to find just the right spot from which to take pictures of wild animals. As with any picture, you have to think about light, obstructions, and the angle of your shot, but if you are taking a picture of a kudu or a parrot, you also have to try not to scare your subject. And if you are taking a picture of a lion, you have to consider your own safety. Fortunately, in zoos you can photograph without fear because a fence, moat, or cage protects you from dangerous animals. But these protections keep the animals a distance away from you, which means they will look too small if you use a normal camera to photograph them. For most of the pictures in this book, I used special telephoto lenses; these act like telescopes so the pictures look like I was right next to the animals, even though I was standing far away.

When there's no barrier preventing me, I sometimes like to get very close, especially with small animals. I use special attachments called macro lenses, which let me focus very close to my subject. I used macro lenses to get big photos of tiny newts and close-up shots of lizard skin. If you use a macro lens, be sure your subject is cooperative, though, or you might get your lens bit off!

I used about two hundred rolls of film while shooting for this book. Each roll has thirty-six exposures, which means that I made about seven thousand photographs to find the fifty-six pictures I chose to include here. The images I was looking for had to be mysterious enough so you'd have to guess what animal was represented, and they had to be interesting enough so you'd want to take the time to guess.

The pictures in this book are tinted brown and white. This is because they were made with black-and-white film and printed on paper made for color photography. The paper created the brown tints. In the early days of photography—more than one hundred years ago—brown-and-white photographs were very popular. I like their warmth and their mystery. The creatures seem both familiar and foreign at the same time.

Watching animals while you wait for a photograph can be very peaceful and is almost always fascinating. I can watch all day while a shark swims back and forth in a predictable pattern. The same goes for a cheetah as he paces. I try to capture that fleeting moment when the shark glides by and looks me in the eye or when the cheetah sits up at the sound of the dinner truck approaching.

As I watch and wait, I listen to others around me discuss the animals in human terms. "Look at that," they say. "He's smiling at us!" Or, "She's bored, poor thing!" Or (giggling), "Doesn't that ostrich look like Uncle Ben?" In some ways animals do resemble humans, but I believe they are very much their own creatures. And that's what I have tried to capture in these pictures.

05-02

E   Horenstein, Henry
         A is for --?

GAYLORD RG